John Wesley's "Perfection" Questions

Theodore R. Weber

Mudie Press
Atlanta, GA

Theodore R. Weber/Mudie Press
MudiePress@gmail.com

Book Layout ©2013 BookDesignTemplates.com

Ordering Information:
POD, kindle, and audio books available at amazon.com

John Wesley's "Perfection" Questions/Theodore R. Weber.
ISBN 978-0-9965191-0-6

CONTENTS

To Rob, in his ministry

After all, the expectation is to be made perfect, not to make yourself perfect. What you are expecting is a work of grace, not a work of self-realization.

TRW

Introduction

"WHEN YOU STAND BEFORE your bishop and annual conference seeking admission to Full Connection in the ministry of the United Methodist Church, you will be asked nineteen questions. They have to do with your personal faith, acceptance of Methodist doctrine and polity, ministerial practice, monetary indebtedness, and seriousness about spending yourself and your time entirely in the work of God. Three of the questions pertain to Wesleyan teaching concerning Christian perfection and your personal engagement with it. All of these questions were authorized by John Wesley for eighteenth-century Methodist preachers. They have not been changed in the interim, and are not likely to be changed. The answer to all of them is 'Yes.' Not 'No' or 'I'll think about it' or 'Hmm' or 'Maybe' or 'You can't be serious!'—but 'Yes.' Begin now to prepare yourselves to give informed and truthful answers to these questions."

More or less, that is what I have said across many years to students in my course on "John Wesley's Ethics"—offered to fulfill the disciplinary requirement for study in Methodist theology in preparation for United Methodist ordination. I have required them to reflect and meditate on all of the questions, but I have been most rigorous in pressing their encounter with the three questions on Christian perfection:

"Are you going on to perfection?"

"Do you expect to be made perfect in love in this life?"

"Are you earnestly striving after it?"

My reasons for this emphasis were mainly two. First, these three questions bring to expression the heart of John Wesley's evangelical theology—recovering the moral image of God, making faith active in love, having the mind that is in Christ Jesus, being led by the Spirit to love as God loves, trusting in grace to bring our loving efforts to fulfillment. Students of Wesley's thought need to work through these questions as dimensions of Christian faith and life and also as windows on the general theological position itself. Second, candidates for membership in Full Connection in the Annual Conference need to be able to answer these questions in the affirmative with integrity, and to do so not only with knowledge of what they mean but also with confidence that they have addressed satisfactorily whatever theological problems they embody.

My concern with these matters arises not only out of my responsibilities and involvements as a seminary professor, and from my personal experience many years ago of having to answer the questions as a candidate for Full Connection, but also from decades of experience in talking with candidates and observing their reactions when the questions are asked in a live setting. There is notable levity—sighs and chuckles—when the bishop asks, "Are you in debt so as to embarrass you in your work?" There are good intentions but varying degrees of mental reservation when he or she confronts them with Wesley's compulsive insistence that his preachers always be diligent, never unemployed (i.e., in their ministerial calling), never "triflingly employed." (What—No golf? No fishing? No vacations at the beach? No TV couch potato time?) But there usually is a pall of uncertainty when the perfection questions are posed.

When these three questions are asked the responses of candidates are by no means uniform. There is an evident mixture of military-style reporting (salute, and sound off!), evasiveness, hesitant mumbling, and thoughtful and informed affirmation. Some candidates bark the expected responses, whether from conviction or indoctrination, or from the desire to stay on course by giving the right answers. Some breeze through because they think of it as just another hoop to jump through on the way to ordination and appointment. Some answer "yes" because they characteristically suck up to authority and will say anything to please those who hold some power over them. (I predict, with regret, that the latter will become popular preachers, and will hold positions of prominence and influence without ever having the guts to challenge anyone with the painful and sacrificial truth of the Gospel.) Some are well and thoughtfully prepared, and answer the questions affirmatively and with conviction. Others will continue to wrestle—faithfully and honestly—with their doubts. Some of them may give up and drop out. A few, however, will mumble something that sort of sounds like "yes," and will hope to work things out in the context of a committed and caring ministry.

Bishops often sense the uncertainty of candidates over the perfection questions, and at times seem unsure themselves. I have seen bishops read through the questions as though the interrogation were merely a ritual, not noticing—or seeming to notice—the reticence of some candidates. On one occasion where I was present, a distinguished bishop paused after the first perfection question and sternly reminded the nervous supplicants that the answer was "YES." On another occasion, a bishop arrived at the perfection questions, chuckled audibly, and said, "This doesn't really mean *perfect!*" Evidently others have taken note of these variations in episcopal practice. The preface to the nineteen questions now includes this instruction: "At the time of the examination the bishop shall also explain to the conference the historic nature of the following questions and seek to interpret their spirit and intent." That instruction to bishops was not included in the disciplinary text when I stood before Bishop Paul Martin on a June afternoon in 1950 with several other candidates to answer the nineteen questions, and to be admitted into Full Connection in the Louisiana Annual Conference. We were on our own, except for what we might have learned in a single course on Methodism in seminary, and from our own reading and listening.

This book is a study of Mr. Wesley's three "Christian Perfection" questions. It is intended both to expound the meanings of the questions and to address the uncertainties and anxieties which many candidates for Full Connection bring to the experience of having to answer them. It is appropriate also for clergy who have been through the process and answered the questions. Some appointed preachers have told me that, having stood before the bishop and the Conference and answered appropriately, they want to get a clearer idea now of what they should have known when they gave an affirmative answer! And, of course, some laity may want to read it in order to try to understand what their preachers are talking about when they sermonize about Methodist perfectionism (if they ever do!). The book is not written for specialists in the field of John Wesley's theology, although of course they are welcome to read it, and to recommend it to their students if they find it useful. It adds nothing new by way of Wesley scholarship, but hopes to communicate a basic understanding of Wesley's thought on these topics.

As a teacher in a United Methodist seminary for thirty-nine years, and especially in my course on John Wesley's Ethics, I have pushed my Methodist students to study the sources and to work through the problems before they have to face a Board of Ministry and stand before their bishop and Annual Conference. I have lectured on the questions, in class and in pastors' conferences. In my seminary courses I have required students to write papers on the perfection questions, not only to understand what they mean but also to face frankly and honestly the issues that trouble some of the students. I am not looking for right answers in these papers, but for evidence that the inquirers recognize implicit theological problems and have struggled with them. That is what I am hoping for also in the readers of this book.

The underlying issues are, what do the perfection questions mean? Why do some persons of deep conviction and commitment find them theologically problematical, if not downright objectionable? What do we learn in the process of thinking through the meanings and the challenges? How does what we learn through research, reflection, and intellectual struggle shape our living and proclaiming of the Gospel of Jesus Christ?

Let me make clear, however, that the book is not a substitute for broad, concentrated, and inquisitive study of John Wesley's theology and ethics. In no sense does it take the place of solid courses on the topic. And no one should bypass the reading of Wesley himself, such as his *A Plain Account of Christian Perfection* and "The Character of a Methodist," and also the really outstanding works on his thought. At the head of the list are Theodore Runyon's *The New Creation: John Wesley's Theology Today*[1], Randy Maddox's *Responsible Grace: John Wesley's Practical Theology*[2], and the much older but still authoritative *Wesley and Sanctification*[3], by Harald Lindstrom. And there are others—not listed here. I note also that Bishop Ernest Lyght has written a book on all nineteen of the questions, published by Abingdon (2015) under the title, *Have you faith in Christ?* Bishop Lyght's book will be useful to candidates in that it covers the full list of questions. However, by contrast with this book it gives rather limited treatment to Wesley's three "perfection" questions.

[1] Nashville: Abingdon, 1998.
[2] Nashville: Kingswood Books, 1994.
[3] London: Epworth Press, n.d.

[1]

John Wesley's Project

WE CANNOT APPROACH the three "perfection" questions without first considering Wesley's more inclusive project, which is the recovery of the image of God. Wherever one reads in Wesley's sermons and other works, one will find him stating over and again that the basic purpose of religion is the recovery of the whole image of God. Image of God defines human nature in its original and ideal form. This image is the capacity to love as God loves. It is not an inherent capacity, but a reflection in human being of the perfections of God, of what Wesley called the "imitable perfections," that is, of God's love, mercy, and justice. It is not a reflection of those perfections belonging to God alone, namely, omnipotence, omniscience, and omnipresence. God remains God, and human beings remain human. However, human beings are fully human only by reason of their relationship to God. At times Wesley used the metaphor of the mirror to express this reflective character. His central point was to communicate that the image of God in human nature was a relational reality that depended on the maintenance of a right relationship with God. It was present in faith, obedience, and trust. So long as this right relationship was maintained, so long did humankind bear this divine image. When the relationship was broken, the imaging relationship, and therefore the capacity to love as God loves, was lost.

The problem which evoked the "Wesley project," as I have called it, is that the creative and enabling pattern of dependence in fact has been broken. Humankind has turned away from God in disobedience and unbelief, or in more general terms, in sin. The right relationship with God is no more. The mirror has been shattered. Human beings no longer have the capacity to love as God loves. What follows in consequence is the disruption of the order of creation, of the ordering of human lives, of the right orientation of the self. There can be no righteousness in the human self and in society unless and until the image of God is recovered and restored. The recovery of the image of God is John Wesley's project. It defines his ministry, and is central to his evangelism and preaching. Christian perfection denotes both the goal of this project and the nature and direction of its process. The recovery of the image of God is the purpose of the three questions.

The recovery of the divine image is a work of divine grace, not of human effort and ingenuity. John Wesley discovered this truth the hard way, namely, by using rigorous moral and spiritual disciplines in a failed attempt to please

God and thereby restore the shattered relationship. In this endeavor he was prompted and encouraged by some of the most influential "spiritual" writers available to him, especially William Law, Jeremy Taylor, and Thomas á Kempis. He developed an exemplary life, but did not find the assurance of divine favor. The Aldersgate experience gave him that assurance, in that he became convinced that the grace of God in Christ was given for the sins of the world, to be sure, but also and especially for his own sins. Whether Aldersgate in fact was the turning point in his life is an argument of some persistence among Wesley scholars, but there is no doubt that he experienced the assurance of divine acceptance set forth in his famous story. The central point here is that salvation is by grace through faith, and is not to be earned by rigorous spiritual exercises and works of the law. That does not mean he dispensed with such exercises and works. To the contrary, he saw them as necessary responses to the saving love of God, but he did not identify them as the path leading to salvation. More about that later, when we inquire into the meaning of the three "perfection" questions.

A further note on the meaning of the "whole image of God." Ultimately, Wesley thought of the image in three forms: the moral, the natural, and the political. I shall refrain from describing and differentiating the three, because Wesley did not acknowledge this typology until 1757, when he was fifty-four years old, and had completed the development of his understanding of Christian perfection. His first notice of this typology was in a quotation from *Ruin* and *Recovery of Man* (1745), by the famous Reformed hymn writer, Isaac Watts. Wesley cited Watts' usage in a footnote to his *The Doctrine of Original Sin, According to Scripture, Reason, and Experience.* He simply cited Watts' use of the three images, without expounding or commenting on them. His only exposition came in two sermons—"The New Birth" (No. 45, 1760), and "The General Deliverance" (No. 60, 1782). In those sermons he began some development of their meaning for him, but never revised his developed theology to account for their implications. There is no mention of the three images even in his *A Plain Account of Perfection*, which he revised for the final time in 1777.

For our present purposes—expounding the notion of a "Wesley Project" underlying the analysis of the three perfection questions—we connect only with what he later would call the "moral image," that is, the capacity to love as God loves. However, any further development of theology in the Wesleyan tradition should draw heavily on all three, and especially on the political image of God.

THE ORDER OF SALVATION

What then was the path, and what was the salvation to which it led? Wesley scholars argue over whether the path should be called the "order of salvation" (*"ordo salutis"*) or the "way of salvation" (*"via salutis"*). The value of the former is that it identifies basic elements of the process leading to salvation. They are the awakening to sin and to separation from God, justification (or forgiveness of sins), the new birth, and sanctification (restoration of the capacity love as God loves). Each step is enabled by grace of a particular kind: prevenient, justifying, sanctifying. The value of the latter term (i.e., the "way of salvation") is that it sees the whole movement towards salvation as a process, and avoids any temptation to see it chopped up into successive steps. Grace of whatever relevant kind is present and operable throughout the whole process. Let us keep both "order" and "path" in mind, because both are true and true to Wesley, but we shall proceed to offer a brief explanation of the elements in the "order." At every step we shall identify the nature of the divine grace that enables the movement. However, here we employ the term "order of salvation," in order to identify the elements in the process.

HELPLESSNESS, AND PREVENIENT GRACE

In the condition of loss of the image of God, which is the native condition of all humankind following the sin of Adam, no one is sufficiently enlightened to recognize that the fundamental problem is loss of the right relationship to God. Nor does anyone have the freedom and the power to restore the relationship. The answer to this problem is the light of God which enlightens everyone who comes into this world. In Wesleyan terms (and in other traditions which use the same concept), it is called *prevenient* grace. The term *prevenient* requires some explanation, not only because it is an unfamiliar word, but also because in the older literature it is called "preventing" grace. "Preventing" makes it sound as though it were keeping us from doing something, whereas the reverse is true. The explanation is that it is taken from Latin words which mean "to come before." This grace is the divine power which both opens our eyes to our condition and offers us the possibility of entering into a restored relationship. It is irresistible grace, but only in the sense that it requires us to see our problems of separation and to recognize the divinely-offered possibility for recovery. It is resistible in the sense that the choices of acceptance or non-acceptance are set before us, but not imposed on us.

This provision separates Wesley from John Calvin and the traditional Calvinists. Wesley agreed with Calvin that all humankind was under the power of sin, and had no inherent capability of self-deliverance. That is what he meant when he declared that "there is not a hair's breadth of difference between us and the Calvinists." Where they disagreed was in Wesley's belief that prevenient grace opened the possibility of salvation to everyone, whereas strict Calvinists believed that salvation was entirely a work of grace. Some persons were elected to eternal salvation, and others to eternal damnation. These Calvinists saw no injustice in this apparently arbitrary election, because all sinners justly were condemned to hell, but God—in God's inexplicable mercy—had chosen some for undeserved salvation. There is no need here for further explanation of this difference, except to refute the old notion that "Calvinists believe in election but Methodists believe in free will." The first claim is true, but the second is not. Wesleyans believe that the will is in bondage to sin, but is set free by grace to accept the gracious offer. The offer is made to everyone.

There is prevenient grace for all of sinful humankind, but no election to either salvation or damnation. Freedom to respond to God is a gift of grace. Such freedom is not a natural capability. It is not "free will" in that sense.

In this regard let us report that when *The Methodist Hymnal* was being revised, a person with a disabling injury appeared before the committee and asked that one of the verses be stricken from the republication of Charles Wesley's great hymn "O, For a Thousand Tongues." The verse was "Hear him ye deaf, his praise ye dumb, your loosened tongues employ. Ye blind, behold your savior come! And leap ye lame for joy!" The justifiable complaint was that the disablements were bad enough; the hymn should not call attention to them. Moreover, the use of the term "dumb" to refer to speech incapacity was confusing, and might lead some persons to suppose that those who did not respond to grace were simply stupid! The committee declined to omit the verse, but nevertheless marked it with an asterisk, suggesting that the verse could be omitted when singing. Even the asterisk provision was wrong, however, because Charles Wesley was using the images to refer only to spiritual impairments, and not at all to physical impairments. The point was that prevenient grace would enable us to see the impairments for what they were—signs of separation from God and of spiritual incapacity—and to embrace the offer of divine healing and liberation. We should note also, that the curings of these disabilities are signs of the messianic age. When Messiah comes, such cures will take place. The verse indeed should be sung in services of worship—with deep conviction!

Prevenient grace is basic Wesleyan/Methodist doctrine. It is the goodness of God always going before us to set us free and to enable us to respond to what God offers us in our helplessness. It is the pillar of cloud by day and the pillar of fire by night. It is always present, because God is always present. It is the power of the Holy Spirit in our baptism, which, after all, is efficacious not because of the sanctity of the officiating clergy, or the purity and authority of the church's rite, but because of the presence and power of the Spirit of God coming before any awareness of need on our part--to call us into the family of Christ. It is the continuing power of divine presence in our lives as we seek to be faithful servants and disciples. Prevenient grace is an "eye opener" in the best sense, as well as a vision of deliverance from sin.

JUSTIFICATION, AND JUSTIFYING GRACE

Justification, in biblical terms, means that God in Christ has forgiven all our sins. There no longer is any barrier between us and God. Because of the merits of Christ we are free to approach the throne of grace without any price in our hands—no need on our part to bargain for our acceptance. We are considered just before God, purely because of the forgiving grace of God in Christ and not by reason of any meritorious works on our part. This is the true meaning of "evangelical." The *evangelion* in this case is the good news that God through Christ has opened the possibility for us to stand before God without needing to make excuses, without having to plead our cases, without working to enable our salvation. By grace through faith we are justified. That is all that it means. The good news of justification is "evangelical" in that sense and only in that sense, and has nothing else to do with modern, conservative "evangelicalism," which at times involves the imposition of new laws.

Like many other theological writers, John Wesley tended to equate justification with reconciliation. See, for example, the concluding sentence of his Sermon No.5, "Justification by Faith": "Believe in the Lord Jesus; and thou, even thou, art reconciled to God." In my opinion, that equation is not correct. Justification is necessary to reconciliation by removing the barriers of sinfulness and sin. It is an essential step to reconciliation with God because it takes away what stands in the way of restoration of the lost image of God. But reconciliation with God implies recovery of the full image of God, that is, restoration of the right relationship, not simply removal of the barriers to restoration.

Wesley had a better opportunity than most others to eliminate this objection, because he understood justification to be a necessary step in the process of salvation, but different from sanctification. "This is sanctification; which is indeed in some degree the immediate fruit of justification, but nevertheless is a distinct gift of God, and of a totally different nature. The one implies what God does for us through his Son; the other what he works in us by his Spirit." (5.II.1). Wesley rightly maintained the distinction between justification and sanctification, but seemed to overlook the point that reconciliation with God implied the restoration of the image of God. Justification does not restore the image of God. Justification is a condition of sanctification and in that respect is necessary to reconciliation. It is the removal of the barrier to restoration, but not itself the restoration of the lost image.

THE NEW BIRTH

The new birth is an element in the order or way of salvation. It is a fundamental change in the orientation of life from whatever has been one's driving commitment to this point, to faithful obedience showing love to God and neighbor. To be "born anew" does not require being zapped psychologically by the Holy Spirit, or having a "road to Damascus" experience—although something like that may be the point of departure. Essentially it means living from God in the light of God with dependence on God for our active present and our humanly undefined future. The important thing is not whether one can identify a moment or date of transition, but whether one is running on a track grounded in faith and aiming towards fulfillment in love.

One shifts to that track when one accepts justification—the forgiveness of sins—through faith in the mercies of God given in Christ. Justification and the new birth occur together in the history of one's salvation, but they are not the same. Justification is necessary to remove the sinful barrier we have erected between ourselves and God. The new birth initiates our struggle with "the power of cancelled sin," that is, with the continuing influence over our choices of the accumulated sins and sinful habits which are not banished from our dispositions even though they no longer stand between us and a right relationship with God. The sins may have been cancelled as guilt barriers to God, but they continue in our ways of thinking and acting and prompt us to sin new. The new birth fights them—by keeping us on track. The new birth also acknowledges the "bent to sinning" (to use another of Charles Wesley's phrases) and enters the self into an unrelenting struggle with it. This "bent" is a persistent tendency, deriving from the original sin of the first parents, to get off the track of love of God and neighbor and return to the demanding motive power of the love of self. The "bent to sinning" is present in all humankind and always resists the recovery of the whole image of God. The new birth acknowledges these challenges and engages them.

John Wesley agreed that justification and entire sanctification might occur in the same person at the same time, but he seemed to feel that any such occurrence was an exception to the usual pattern of movement in faith along the order or way of salvation. The new birth with its "track" towards sanctification therefore was—for him—representative of normative Christian experience. And the more the new birth keeps us on that track, that is, the more we grow into the love of Christ, the more successful we become in fighting the temptations to sin.

SANCTIFICATION

Sanctification is the final element in the *ordo salutis*, or way of salvation. It is the condition of holiness, or the internalization of the love of God known most fully in Jesus Christ. In its completeness as the goal of the Christian life it is the full recovery of the lost image of God. As indicated, it is the goal of those who have faith in Christ, and are called to live their lives close to God, following Gods' commandments. It is also the path of the Christian life—the unending process of those who have committed their lives in faith and continue to grow in the holiness of divine love. I stress *unending*, because the process of growing more loving begins in this life and moves on eternally into the next.

One must keep these distinctions in mind if someone asks, "Have you been saved?" What the questioner is asking is whether something has happened in your conscious life to rescue you from hell and assure you of a future with God in heaven. That is an appropriate concern, but it is not what Wesley meant by salvation in its fullest sense. For Wesley, salvation was the process of restoration of the full image of God. It was the entire course of the Christian life, not simply a moment of faithful commitment. That one should have assurance of being in the presence of God for eternity was of great importance to him, and it came to expression in his evangelistic work. But for him the reality of salvation was the process that begins in this life and continues into the next. Salvation is eternal growth in the love of Christ, not simply the moment when one knows forgiveness of sins and accepts it in faith. The latter he called justification. It is a necessary step in the way of salvation, but by no means the whole of it. The Wesley Project was the recovery and renewal of the image of God—a continuing process in faith, not only a moment of rescue.

Consider in this regard the meaning of Jesus' response to the lawyer who asked what he must do to inherit eternal life. Jesus asked him what was written in the law, and he replied, "You shall love the Lord your God with all your heart, and with all your soul, and with all your strength, and with all your mind: and your neighbor as yourself." Jesus assured him that was the right answer, and if he did that he would live. (Luke 10:25-28, NSRV). The implication of the response, however, is that commitment to love in such unreserved fashion would supplant the self-interest in eternal life, and replace it with self-giving love. To do what was necessary for eternal life would transform the quest from self to God and the neighbor. Commitment in love, and growth in love are what give life, but they also remove anxiety about the self from the center of concern. That is what John Wesley meant by sanctification. The more one moved on the track towards sanctification the less anxiety there would be, because increasingly the movement would take the self out of the center.

As one can see, the Wesley project—the recovery of the capacity to love as God loves—requires a moment of awareness and conversion, but it is a total process not limited to that one moment. It is the process of sanctification—of growing closer to Christ in holiness—which includes the dawning awareness of sin, the acceptance in faith of divine justification, and the new birth in Christ—all in the course of being directed by grace through faith to recover the lost image of God. That is John Wesley's understanding of salvation. It is a process, not a single causative and illuminating moment—although such may and will occur. The process begins in this life and continues in the next. It is enabled and guided by several forms of divine grace: prevenient, justifying, sanctifying. These forms have different descriptive names, but all of them point to the activity of the Holy Spirit of God in the life of those who have come to faith in Christ.

[2]

The Three "Perfection" Questions

ARE YOU GOING ON TO PERFECTION?

WHAT IS BEING ASKED HERE? What are the problems, if any? What are the reasons for a positive response?

First, it is evident that the question is referring to a process—something that is moving along, proceeding to a goal. In that sense, it matches what I have said previously—that Wesley looked upon perfection/salvation as a process. Second, the goal is *perfection*, which needs to be understood as Wesley defined it. Third, the question focuses on the person being addressed—on *you*. Are you personally in this process? If so, where are you, and how do you understand what is happening, what you are doing, and where you are going?

However, before we even get to this question, and indeed to all the others, there is a first question which candidates for Full Connection must answer: Have you faith in Christ? Deal with this question first. Then and only then will you be able to give truthfully affirmative answers to the others. Remember, of course, that when John Wesley spoke of "having faith" he meant trusting Christ for your salvation and guidance, in other words, leaning your whole life and future on him. Of course, he also meant believing in Christ, his divine-human reality, his place in the holy Trinity, and his saving power. But he gave priority to faith as trust, because he did not want to allow faith in Christ to be merely an intellectual and doctrinal commitment with no surrender and wholeheartedness to support it.

I would suppose that most if not all of the candidates who hear this question adhere at minimum to the doctrinal commitment to Christ. If they don't, they probably would not think themselves ready to stand before their conference and their bishop and face the questioning. They will have some questions about particular doctrinal items, but they are working on them in a context of basic belief. But each must ask him- or herself, do I really trust Christ for my salvation? Do I come singing, "Nothing in my hand I bring, simply to thy cross I cling?" Do I trust nothing else for salvation—nation, race, family, school, teachers, pastors, my own abilities, fawning praise of church members—but Christ ultimately and Christ alone? If they have doctrinal belief in Christ, but not life-surrendering trust, perhaps they should review the memorable advice of Peter Boehler to young

John Wesley in his time of self-doubt: "Preach faith until you have it. Then because you have faith, you will preach faith." That advice may be a bit too flippant, but there is truth in it. If one is committed to Christ through faith in a doctrinal sense, one can confront and work through many occasions of doubt, and because one is on the right track doctrinally, one may be given the grace to trust. Bear in mind, of course, that faith as trust usually is not given all at once in one big cosmic zap. It develops through time and many trials. But in any event the first question stands before the others: Do you have faith in Christ?

With that necessity at hand, let us consider the process (going on") implied in the question. It has been set out already in discussing the Wesley Project. The process explicitly is the order of salvation—or way of salvation, if you prefer. The elements of the order are awakening, justification, the new birth, and sanctification. It is a *way* of salvation, because the elements of the order are not disconnected or simply successive. The prospect and calling of sanctification are present from the beginning of the process, and they connect with and attend all the other elements of the order.

The process includes awakening to one's status in sin, to the need of salvation, and to the grace of forgiveness available to us before we ever ask for it. Accepting the gift of forgiveness, and thereby removing the barrier between ourselves and God, is what Wesley meant by *justification*. It is indeed a gift, because it is provided to us by God's love. It is not something that we either earn or possibly could earn. It is available to us because of God's sacrifice for us in Jesus Christ. We receive it by faith—by our faith in the power and love of God and in the saving presence of God in Christ. The word of grace accepted through faith is, "Your sins are forgiven."

If you hear that word, and accept its forgiveness in faith, you are moving along in the process towards sanctification. But note: justification is not a one-time event, even though the first experience of it may have a special place in the memory of our faith journey. The "bent to sinning" is ever with us. We struggle every moment against the temptations to sin, and we do not always win. Therefore we need the forgiving, justifying grace of God through Christ in every moment. That is one of the reasons why we must acknowledge our placement in a process of "going on."

The second aspect of this process is the goal. Are you going on to *perfection*, that is, to a perfection of love like that of Christ? Let us look ourselves over and be sure that perfection is our goal in a life committed to ministry. The goal is not to be a "successful" minister, by worldly standards, nor to become a "great preacher" (although compelling, inspiring preaching certainly should be one of our aims), nor to get a "better" church in every appointment, nor to be a D.S. or a bishop (although if our fundamental goal is the love of Christ, and we are called to one of those offices, we shall exercise it with loving, pastoral care). Remember always, and in every moment, relationship, and station of ministry that the question to which you are responding is whether you are going on to perfection.

And so, are you ready to give an affirmative answer to the question—because you are on the right track, and by faith and grace are moving along?-

DO YOU EXPECT TO BE MADE PERFECT IN LOVE IN THIS LIFE?

The usual first-out-of the-gate response to this question is, "No. I don't really expect that." Doubtless that is a proper exercise in humility. We don't think we actually are capable of achieving such heights, and we don't want to pretend to such capability—or lie about our real expectations. But let us think theologically about the question. If we are confronting it with an assessment of our own abilities, then the only right answer is—no. But if we think about it with reference to the enabling and empowering grace of God, then the right answer is—yes. That is one reason why the prior question about having faith in Christ is so important. If you have faith in Christ—if you really *trust* in Christ—then you know that power not reducible to or equated with your own aptitudes is engaged actively in bringing you to that result. After all, the expectation is *to be made perfect*, not to make yourself perfect. What you are expecting is a work of grace, not a work of self-realization. As a person with faith in Christ, do you trust the divine power to make that happen? No? Or yes?

Let us remember at the outset that Wesley did not mean perfection in everything. He did not mean that we would have no bodily infirmities, that we would know everything, and that we would be free of mistakes. Also, he did not expect us to imitate God in the ways God could not be imitated. Our expectation is to be made perfect *in love*. That is a very important specification, because John Wesley in fact had two definitions of perfection, not just one. One specification is the perfection of Christ's love. It is to love as God loves. To love in that way is to experience the restoration of a right relationship with God. It is the recovery of the image of God. A second specification is the avoidance of sin. "A Christian is in so far perfect as not to commit sin." Sin, in this understanding, is "the willful violation of any known law." That specification, of course, is much more problematical. If we were to take this requirement in its absolute sense, we never would be able to disobey unjust laws—which we shall confront quite certainly and unavoidably in the course of ministerial service. No challenge to laws enforcing racial segregation, gender discrimination, etc. Nor would we be allowed even to disregard or disobey laws that are simply unwise, or have lost their relevance with the passing of time. John Wesley himself did not always obey "any known law." He defied the laws of the church to preach in the open fields, to use spontaneous prayer, and to sing hymns that were not in the hymnal. Moreover, he followed Calvin and other theologians in explaining away the binding character of the harshest or least relevant laws of the Old Testament. Some of those laws were set aside because they were considered to be ceremonial or ritual laws binding on the Hebrew people in a particular era. The law binding on everyone was the moral law, expressed permanently and universally in the Ten Commandments. For these *moral* laws Wesley allowed no exception.

Of course, he took the matter of obedience to law with great seriousness. He was a law-abiding man himself, and he expected his Methodists to be law-abiding citizens and church members. Perhaps that explains the emphasis. However, he knew and cited the Scripture passage from Acts 5:29: "We must obey God rather than men." Across the centuries the church had cited this Scripture to set limits to obedience to law and political authority. For Wesley, as for the historic church, obedience to God trumped all other forms of obedience, however legitimate they might be otherwise. Nevertheless, in this question to prospective conference members he was thinking of perfection only in the first sense: "Do you expect to be made perfect *in love...*?" When he bound his preachers in a commitment to seek perfection, he clearly meant the perfection of love, an achievement empowered and delivered by the grace of God received through faith. And he taught also that the greater the maturation in Christian love, the stronger would be the capability to struggle against the temptations to sin.

But do you expect to be made perfect even in love alone *in this life*? The first response, and in this sense a correct one, is to answer no—for a Wesleyan reason. The reason, as we have observed, is that the perfection of love never stops growing, even in the next life—or perhaps especially there. That is true, but it is not a sustainable objection. What Wesley meant is that the love of Christ should replace the "bent to sinning" at the center of the self, and do so entirely. That would be the perfection of love. In his view it would be attainable in this life, although it would continue throughout eternity to deepen in its richness. Do you expect to be made perfect in that sense?

John Wesley thought that was possible and that it should happen. Curiously, he never claimed it for himself, and his emphasis on this result seemed to have been a passing phase. Seemingly at war with this desired result, even in his own thinking, were other considerations. One was that the perfection of love cannot be a permanent, personal possession. Unlike those who argue "once saved, always saved," John Wesley believed such perfection could be lost. He feared that if his followers thought otherwise they might take pride in their status. Such pride would be evidence that they had not in fact reached the perfection of love. Another was that the temptations of sin never went away, and the risks of succumbing to those temptations were always present to test the perfection of love.

We must point out also that Wesley did not have a concept of the self as social. By that I mean the analysis of the self as existing at the confluence of many different relationships, each of which makes some contribution to selfhood.[4] Given that understanding, one never can see the self as totally free of sin, because one participates in the sinfulness of the relationships, including those of the structure and institutions in which one exists. It is true that Wesley insisted that there were no solitary Christians, and that in this sense the self was social, but all he meant by that was that Christians needed the fellowship and nurturing of small groups. When he spoke of what came to be called entire sanctification, he was thinking of the person in individual terms, not as a person existing in reality at the center of relationships. The latter understanding cannot sustain a notion of personal perfection in this life. The injustices of the relationships in which we stand are injustices in which we participate.

How then can one answer "yes" to this question? First of all, we must remember that the expectation is grounded in the efficacy of grace, not in confidence in one's own spiritual achievement. If we fulfill this expectation, it is because of the work of God in us, not because of the prospect of personal achievement. An affirmative answer means that we are affirming the presence and power of divine grace, not any assessment of our own meritorious prospects. Second, if grace is at work in our decisions and actions, there indeed may be times when we act in the perfection of love, possibly even counter to our own awareness, and counter to the social pressures to conform. Once again, if we can answer "yes" to this question, it is because with faith in Christ we can trust in the promise of divine grace.

ARE YOU EARNESTLY STRIVING FOR IT?

When considering this question we must bear in mind that early in his career John Wesley had a serious disagreement with some persons whose friendship and religious views he otherwise treasured. These persons believed sincerely that salvation was by grace through faith, and that given that conviction they should sit quietly and wait for the Holy Spirit to visit them and lead them. In other words, they should do nothing of a constructive, helpful nature unless and until the Spirit moved them to do so. Wesley agreed strongly with the notion of salvation by grace through faith, but he disagreed at least as strongly with the further inference that as Christians they should take no action—even loving ones—not urged upon them directly by the movement of that Spirit. In his view, works of active love were binding upon Christians. Christians should do "good works." They should be "earnestly striving" to express their love more fully and to develop their capacity to love as God loves, that is, to move towards full recovery of the lost image of God. If they knew the love of Christ, and if they were on the track towards Christian perfection, they would of course express their commitments in concrete acts of love towards the neighbor.

In his own practice, Wesley offered loving assistance not only to those in his Methodist following, but also to those who suffered loss and vulnerability because of the destructive effects of a rapidly changing society. He had a very deliberate ministry to the poor, including begging money for them even when he was a very old man. He organized what we would call a credit union, provided medical help, visited the prisons, launched a stinging and effective attack on the slave trade and African slavery, and even criticized the concepts and practices of the British economic system. Striving for Christian perfection was not an abstract, individualized process, but a matter of growing in love through practicing concrete acts of love. When he instructed his preachers that "You have nothing to do but save souls," all that he meant was that—as laymen—they should lay aside their remunerative work as farmers, shopkeepers, carpenters, etc., and devote themselves entirely to the preaching of the Word. He clearly did not mean that they should shun the kinds of personal and social ameliorating work in which he himself engaged.

John Wesley agreed that persons who had not experienced faith in Christ could perform worthy acts, and that they would be good for the beneficiaries. What he denied, however, was that such works were good in the sense of earning salvation in the absence of saving faith. To be "Christian" works specifically, they must arise from the liberating gift of faith and be attended by the empowerment of the Holy Spirit. Only with those presuppositions were they evidences of "earnestly striving," of being on the track to the perfection of love. But such works must arise. However, he saw at least two problems, and these problems cause difficulties for Christians of conscience who would like to affirm the call to strive earnestly.

One problem was the risk of imposing a new law— one that would set legal requirements for achieving Christian perfection, rather than allowing the works of service and help to emerge by impulse as a response to divine love. There is no doubt that some of John Wesley's Christians fell into that legalistic trap. In nineteenth-century Methodism, some of the Methodists in their quest for scriptural holiness reduced holiness to the fulfillment of a moral-scriptural law. In the worst instances, they cut the law down to matters of personal morality, such as dancing, drinking alcohol, smoking, fornication, gambling, and the like. The problem was not that they were wrong in stressing standards of personal; morality, but that in itemizing the law thusly they turned their view from larger social sins, such as slavery, segregation, economic injustice, gender discrimination, international belligerence, and the like. The striving for a Christlike expression of Christian love pertains to all forms of human activity, and not only to those which we can master individualistically. Moreover, even with that extended understanding of the law, "earnestly striving" still carries the risk of transforming loving Christian practice into a legalistic exercise. "Earnestly striving" is not a means to earn our way to perfection. It is the practice of responsive love. "We love, because he first loved us."

Another problem was that persons who felt that they were making significant progress in the expression of Christian love might come to feel pretty good about their moral and spiritual achievements. As one of my teachers (young Albert Outler) put it, "He stuck in his thumb and pulled out a plum, and said 'What a good boy am I!'" That is what we call narcissism—looking at one's self approvingly, and praising one's self for what one has become. Narcissism puts the self at the center and lauds it, rather than acknowledging a work of grace and the effective presence of the Holy Spirit. Moreover, this attitude overlooks the risks of momentary and continuing sinfulness, for "sin always lieth at the door."

Not only should Christians always be about the business of doing "good works"—as expressions of responsive love and not as ways of proving their goodness to God or to themselves—but they also should attend on all the ordinances of God—church attendance, prayer, the Holy Communion, and Christian fellowship and conferencing. That is, they should seek to praise God in all the appointed ways. Doing so does not constitute obedience to another law. It reflects the fact that God seeks us out and draws us towards the divine presence. These ways of organizing and expressing the spiritual life are responses to the grace of God that comes before any of our actions. They are movements in response to prevenient grace, not eager efforts to prove ourselves to God. They support and encourage our growth in love.

As means of organizing their own ways of service to others and their more formal practice of the presence of God, Methodist Christians would do well to follow the guidelines of the General Rules of the United Societies, found in your *Discipline*. These rules are: "*First*: By doing no harm, by avoiding evil of every kind....*Secondly*: By doing good; by being in every kind merciful after their power; as they have opportunity, doing good of every possible sort, and, as far as possible, to all....*Thirdly*: By attending upon all the ordinances of God...." The specific ways of following these rules—especially the first two—will need some rethinking in order to apply them to our own time, but the rules themselves are binding as guides, and even many of the specific applications are still relevant. The third one certainly remains in force. I must point out also that as Methodist Christians you should follow and apply these rules, but as pastors you must take care to inform your congregations of them, and to assist the faithful in employing them as their own ways to striving earnestly to respond to the saving love of God.

But note: To follow these rules is to engage in "earnestly striving" for perfection, but it is not a way of earning it. The achievement of the aspiration always is a work of grace, not something for which we ourselves can take credit. The "earnest striving" is to be more Christlike and self-giving in whatever we do for others and for God, not to achieve a particular status which we can carry around and put on display. That must be made clear in our preaching and teaching, as well as in our personal practice. With this understanding of the question we can and should answer it affirmatively.

[3]

Reflections on the Theology of Affirmative Response

TAKE ANOTHER CAREFUL LOOK at the three "perfection" questions. Are you ready to answer—honestly—when the bishop asks them? What do they mean, and what is presupposed? If you can affirm that you are going on to perfection, that means you trust your present and your future to the work of God in Christ and to the presence of the Holy Spirit. It means that you are on the track to let your faith become active in love. The question is not more demanding than that, but the demand is by no means trivial. If you can say that you expect to be made perfect in love in this life you are not puffing yourself up to foresee some heroic exercise of self-realization. You are simply—but powerfully—trusting the grace of God to carry you to a holy result well beyond your own capacities—however great or limited they may be. If you commit yourself to "earnestly striving" for the perfection of Christian love, you are not submitting to a new law of perfectionist achievement, nor are you setting yourself up for an exercise in self-congratulation. Once again, you are trusting in God to make all of your actions in Christian discipleship more loving and more sacrificial than you could make them with your own supposed spiritual commitments. You will do good to others, because that is the Christian way and because God liberates you from self-concern to do so. You will attend on all the ordinances of God, not to demonstrate your spirituality or to curry favor with the Divine One, but simply because God has ordained these means to express gratitude to God and to strengthen your will to love.

CAN YOU DO THAT? AS MINISTERS CAN YOU LEAD OTHERS TO DO THE SAME?

You should not attempt to understand these expectations without knowing something about how John Wesley thought about them. First, John Wesley was a theologian of grace. He believed that the grace of God always was present to open our eyes to understanding our separation from God, and to show us the way to overcome that separation. He spoke of prevenient, justifying, and sanctifying grace, but all of these were nothing more than conceptualizations of the various modes of divine presence and action in the work of salvation. Our entire redemption, and all of our activity as redeemed persons, is a work of God, and God supports us every step of the way. The grace of God is always present. It is active and supportive. As the word indicates, it is free. In the words of the old Methodist hymn, the way of God is "free grace and a dying love." One cannot engage the "perfection" questions outside of a context of grace. Trust in the grace of God is the empowerment for answering them and performing them. We must be theologians of grace, as John Wesley was.

John Wesley was a theologian of love. Love of God and of neighbor is the reconstruction of the image of God. What Wesley was asking of his preachers, and indeed of all his Methodists, was that they follow the prompting of the Holy Spirit to get on the track towards the perfection of love, and stay there, by the grace of God—and not because of their own motivations and capabilities. Love for Wesley was not a warm, fuzzy feeling. It was the true presence of Christ in our lives, the right relationship to God, the directive power in all relationships and in the motive of service to all who are in need. Conversion to Christ is not fire insurance to protect us from the terrors of hell, it is union with the saving love of God that endured the cross for the salvation of the world. That is what those three questions are all about. When you respond to the three questions, think love—love to God, love to the neighbor, love as the recovery of the image of God, love as response to the divine love manifest fully in Christ.

John Wesley was a theologian of freedom. That statement is meant more in a theological sense than in a political sense. We are in bondage to a will turned toward self and against God, but the grace of God sets us free to serve God. We are in bondage to the law of works, anxious if not terrified that we cannot please God and thus win divine favor, but the grace of God turns our motive from self-striving to responsive love. We are in bondage to the lord of this world and the ways of this world, but the death and resurrection of Christ liberate us to obey God rather than men, and to serve the needful neighbor and not the demands and desires of the rich and powerful. That last statement should make it clear, however, that the theological sense of freedom also has political implications. Christians are in the world to serve the poor and the powerless, not to be bought and kept instruments of the mighty and the comfortable. Preachers, beware!

John Wesley was a theologian of decision and development. As an evangelist he preached for decisions. He opened the vision of saving grace to all humankind, to sinners, to whoever was unresponsive to the gifts of forgiveness and renewal, and urged them to make the move to trust in the loving power of deliverance. As a pastor he took care to cultivate the early movements of responsive love of God and neighbor, and to encourage them in the grace-assisted process of growing in love through this life and on into the next. To him, both the occasion of decision and the nurturing of Christian character were essential works of ministry and constitutive elements of the fullness of salvation. Both are implied in affirmative answers to the perfection questions.

As we prepare to answer these questions, do we understand fully that John Wesley's theological orientation must be our own? And are we prepared to answer them rightly, honestly, and without reservation as we pursue our divine calling to commit our lives entirely to the service of God and God's people?

[4] For the most authoritative statement of this position, see H. Richard Niebuhr, *The Responsible Self* (New York: Harper & Row, c. 1963 by Florence M. Niebuhr).

Bibliography

PRIMARY SOURCES

Wesley, John. *A Plain Account of Christian Perfection*. Pp. 366-446, in *The Works of John Wesley*, vol. 9, Jackson ed., 1872 (Grand Rapids: Baker Book House, 1979).

_____. *The Character of a Methodist*, pp. 31-42, in *The Works of John Wesley*, Vol. 9, ed. Rupert E, Davies (Nashville: Abingdon Press, 1989).

SECONDARY SOURCES

Abraham, William J. *Wesley for Armchair Theologians* (Louisville: Westminster John Knox Press, ©2005).

Cobb, John B., Jr. *Grace and Responsibility; A Wesleyan Theology for Today* (Nashville: Abingdon, ©1995).

Collins, Kenneth J. *Wesley on Salvation; A Study in the Standard Sermons* (Grand Rapids: Francis Asbury Press, c. 1989).

Klaiber, Walter, and Manfred Marquardt. *Living Grace: An Outline of United Methodist Theology* (Nashville: Abingdon Press, ©2001).

Lindstrom, Harald. *Wesley and Sanctification* (London: Epworth Press, n.d.)

Maddox, Randy. *Responsible Grace: John Wesley's Practical Theology* (Nashville: Kingswood Books, 1994).

Niebuhr, H. Richard. *The Responsible Self.* (New York: Harper & Row, ©1963, by Florence M. Niebuhr).

Runyon, Theodore H. *The New Creation: John Wesley's Theology Today* (Nashville: Abingdon Press, 1998).

Weber, Theodore R. *Politics in the Order of Salvation; Transforming Wesleyan Political Ethics* (Nashville: Kingswood Books, c. 2001).

Williams, Colin W. *John Wesley 's Theology Today; A Study of the Wesleyan Tradition in the Light of Current Theological Dialogue* (Nashville: Abingdon Press, c. 1960).

Acknowledgments

As I have indicated in the text, for many years I taught the course on "John Wesley's Ethics" in the Candler School of Theology of Emory University. I express my gratitude to the students who participated in those sessions, and especially to those who helped amplify and correct my own understanding of Wesley's theology and ethics. My thanks also to the School of Congregational Development of the North Alabama Conference of the United Methodist Church, whose administrators invited me to Camp Sumatanga to give the lectures on which this booklet is based. Also lecturing at that gathering was my son, Dr. Rob Weber, who arranged the invitations, read the manuscript, and urged me to try e-publishing. To him this work is dedicated. Stacy Hood provided invaluable and dedicated assistance by transcribing the original lectures and preparing the text for publication. My wife, Mudie, always is the indispensable person in my life and work.

About the Author

 Dr. Theodore R. Weber is Professor Emeritus of Social Ethics in the Candler School of Theology of Emory University, where he taught for thirty-nine years. A clergy member (ret.) of the Louisiana United Methodist Annual Conference, Dr. Weber has served pastorates in Louisiana and Connecticut, as acting chaplain of Emory University, and as a member of the ministerial staff of St. Giles Cathedral in Edinburgh, UK. He has lectured and preached widely in the United States, Europe, Hong Kong, Japan, and South Korea. A former president of the Society of Christian Ethics in the U.S. and Canada, he also is author of *Politics in the Order of Salvation; Transforming Wesleyan Political Ethics* (Nashville: Abingdon, c. 2001).

Made in the USA
Lexington, KY
30 November 2015